MEGASTRUCTURES

BUILDINGS

E N T S

Page No.

1. History, Brick by Brick   05

2. The High-Rise Buildings   09

3. Art of Architecture   13

4. Glossary   47

5. Index   48

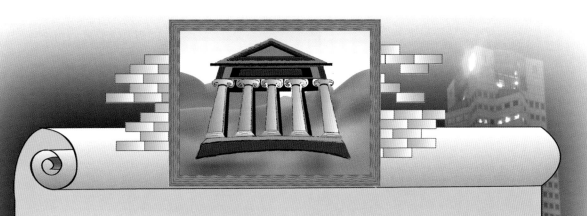

History, Brick by Brick

Though building construction is an ancient activity, it has evolved, moving from simple to complex planning and construction, from horizontal expansion to vertical growth, and from small to megastructures. With the technological progress, the façades of buildings, too have changed in shape, in size and in durability.

The most essential task of building construction is to satisfy one of the most basic of human needs — a roof over one's head. Buildings serve many purposes, and construction is not confined to providing dwellings only. Apart from protecting against the fluctuating climate, a building is a mirror of the society. It depicts the everchanging needs of people.

The construction of tall structures, commonly called skyscrapers, originated from the desire for greater height and span. William Le Baron Jenney (1832–1907) is considered to be the father of modern skyscrapers. After working as a civil engineer in the civil war of 1861, William honed his skill by erecting steel edifices, such as the Home Insurance Office Building (1885) and Ludington Building (1891).

William Le Baron Jenney, the father of modern skyscrapers.

HISTORY, BRICK BY BRICK

Q How have buildings evolved?

A In the beginning, the shelters built by humans were simple and not very durable, lasting only a few days or months. As time passed, the temporary structures evolved into more refined forms like the *Igloo*, and the changes continue to occur.

Q What forms of tent were used in the past?

A Tents such as the Saudi Arabian *goats' hair tent*, the Mongolian *yurt* with its collapsible wooden frame and felt covering and the American–Indian *tepee* with its multiple poles were used in the past.

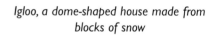
Igloo, a dome-shaped house made from blocks of snow

Q What type of buildings prevailed in the Stone Age?

A During the Stone Age, people moved around a wide area to gather food through hunting. Consequently, they built temporary shelters using circular stones, wooden poles or tents made of animal skin. These structures, though not very durable, helped to protect Stone Age people from rain, snow and sun. The structures also provided them with privacy.

Q How did the agricultural revolution change the façade of buildings?

A Around 10,000 B.C., the agricultural revolution took place, which gave a major boost to the kind of buildings being constructed. The practice of agriculture as a livelihood, confined people to a particular locality–resulting in dwellings that were more permanent than the earlier versions.

Q What was the building material used during the Neolithic period?

A During the Neolithic period, heavy timbers were used in making buildings. However, it was difficult to cut large trees with stone tools. This limited its use as a building material.

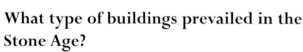

Mongolian Yurt
American Indian tepee
Inner section of Tholoi

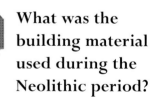

6

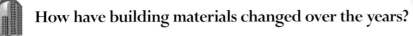

How have building materials changed over the years?

In ancient times, leaves, branches and animal hides were used as building material, all of which were perishable. Then came more durable natural material, such as clay, stone and timber. The need for durability grew more with the desire for stability. This gave rise to building material like brick, concrete, metals and plastics.

What is a 'Tholoi'?

In the villages of the Middle East, remains of round dwellings have been found. These round dwellings are called 'Tholoi'. Tholoi walls are made of packed clay. In Europe, Tholoi was made up of a dry-laid stone with domed roofs.

What led to the adoption of a rectangular plan form in buildings?

A rectangular antechamber was later attached to the circular chamber of the 'Tholoi' in the Middle East. As a rectangular shape was found to be more convenient a construction for

Home Insurance Office Building (1885), Chicago

including more rooms, more dwellings could be placed together in settlements. As a result the rectangular shape came to stay and marked the beginning of masonry construction.

When was the first skyscraper built?

The first skyscraper, the 10-storeyed Home Insurance Office building in Chicago, Illinois was built in 1885. It was built by William Le Baron Jenney. The skyscraper was an iron and steel structure, encased in brick or clay tile shell for protection against fire. The very first skyscraper also had electric passenger elevators.

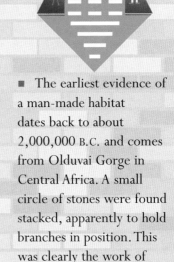

■ The earliest evidence of a man-made habitat dates back to about 2,000,000 B.C. and comes from Olduvai Gorge in Central Africa. A small circle of stones were found stacked, apparently to hold branches in position. This was clearly the work of Homo Habilis, our tool-making ancestor.

■ Archaeologists have discovered the remains of Stone Age houses, 7,000 years back, on an island off-the-coast of the United Arab Emirates.

■ Joseph Aspdin patented the first true artificial cement in 1824, which he called Portland Cement, after the high quality Portland stone.

HISTORY, BRICK BY BRICK

Which is Chicago's earliest surviving skyscraper?

'Ludington Building' is Chicago's earliest surviving skyscraper. It was built in 1891 by Mary Ludington to house the American Book Company. The building, designed by William Le Baron Jenney, is the first skyscraper to be built in terra cota.

Which was Europe's first skyscraper?

The Royal Liver Building built in 1909, in Liverpool, by Hennebique's English representative Louis Mouchel, was Europe's first skyscraper. Its clock tower height was 95 m (311 feet).

Who was the architect of 'Columbus Memorial Building, Chicago'?

William W. Boyington was the main architect of the 'Columbus Memorial Building, Chicago'. Like most of Boyington's buildings, the building has been constructed in the neo-Gothic style. The building was constructed in 1893 and was later destroyed in 1959.

Columbus Memorial Building, (1893), Chicago

Ludington Building (1891), Chicago

Why did the need for the megastructures arise?

With the increase of population in urban areas, the available land for business expansion became scarce. This led to the concept of mega-structures which were designed to conserve the natural environment and to fulfil various human requirements.

The High-Rise Buildings

Touching the sky has always been a human fascination. You have seen spider man swinging on tall towers and buildings. These high-rise buildings are called megastructures.

A high-rise is a special kind of tall building. High-rises are enclosed, multi-storeyed, and serviced by a vertical transportation system (i.e. elevators). A high-rise building is divided into occupiable levels at regular intervals. Examples of high-rises include Toronto's Canadian National Tower, New York's Seagram Building, and Los Angeles's Bank of America Tower.

A high-rise may or may not be a skyscraper. The word 'skyscraper' was originally a nautical term for a tall mast or a sail. But today, the definition of the word has changed. The word is now used to refer to a tall building, usually higher than 152 m (499 feet). Most of the skyscrapers serve as office buildings or hotels. The term 'high-rise' is also used to describe tall buildings, but it tends to be applied specifically to residential buildings.

A few years ago, the skyscraper seemed to have become a very tired 20th century symbol. But now there has been an increase of interest in iconic high-rise buildings.

THE HIGH-RISE BUILDINGS

What makes a mega-high-rise?

Any building will fall into the category of a mega-high-rise, if it exceeds 75 storeys and is equipped with one or more sky lobbies.

Which was the tallest building in Chicago prior to 1920?

The Masonic Temple in Chicago, with a height of 92 m (302 feet), was the tallest building in Chicago prior to 1920. It was constructed in 1892 and contained 21 storeys. Large windows were installed in it from top to bottom to give adequate light to the building. It was later demolished in 1939.

Masonic Temple (1892), Chicago

When did the high-rise race begin in New York?

The high-rise race started with the construction of the 16-storeyed Manhattan Life Building in 1891. Next was the 47-storeyed Singer Building, which was developed by architect Ernest Flagg in 1908. In 1913, the height went up further with the construction of the 57-storeyed Woolworth Building. Eighteen years later, in 1931, a 102-storeyed Empire State Building was constructed. The World War II halted the race for higher structures.

Woolworth Building (1913), New York

What has been Paolo Soleri's contribution in construction of megastructures?

An Italian-born American architect and designer, Paolo Soleri has been credited with building a number of urban mega centres that were raised vertically instead of horizontally on the ground. In 1959, he designed 'Mesa City', a desert city housing about two million people. He coined the term 'Arcology' from 'architecture' and 'ecology' to describe his utopian constructions.

What kind of mega-high-rise projects are being planned now?

Mega-high-rise projects are being planned which will be multi-use complexes or cities within cities. These buildings would have a subterranean parking garage, a retail component, food courts, a supermarket, a movie or an entertainment centre, night clubs or disco or karaoke bars, office space, business or service apartments, residential apartments, a hotel, upper-floor restaurants and a rooftop observation level.

How can high-rise structures be utilised for business?

The retail space of the building should be close to the terminal floor and sky lobby to capture the interest of passersby. Restaurants and observation decks, with spectacular views can also attract customers.

What role does a sky lobby play in a megastructure?

In a megastructure, a sky lobby acts as a transfer point for a double-decker elevator system. Usually it is located in a floor, where a bridge links the identical towers in a megastructure.

When and how is a sky lobby added in a megastructure?

While working out an elevator zone design, usually after 60 storeys, the 5th zone of single deck or the 4th zone of double decks is not added normally, as the elevator shafts take too much of building space. Instead, addition of a sky lobby located above the first set of local zone elevators is considered, which is served by its own express sky lobby shuttles, and then the local service zones are stacked all over again.

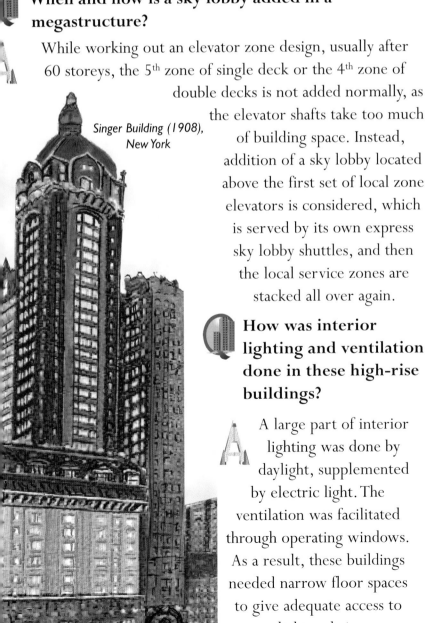

Singer Building (1908), New York

How was interior lighting and ventilation done in these high-rise buildings?

A large part of interior lighting was done by daylight, supplemented by electric light. The ventilation was facilitated through operating windows. As a result, these buildings needed narrow floor spaces to give adequate access to light and air.

THE HIGH-RISE BUILDINGS

When was electric arc welding introduced?

Electric arc welding was introduced in the 1880s, which made a significant impact on the construction industry. However, the first all-welded multi-storeyed buildings were developed for the Westinghouse Company's factories in 1920. Consequently, the use of electric arc became a new structural type for medium spans, reaching a length of 23 m (77 feet) in the Cincinnati Union Terminal in 1932.

What is the comfort level acceleration that elevators should have?

The human body can tolerate acceleration rates of about $0.9–1.5\,m/sec^2$ in a vertical plane without discomfort. The majority of the current high-rise gearless elevator hoist machines are adhering to these limits.

Which is the world's first application of double-deck sky lobby shuttle elevator?

'Sears Tower in Chicago', is the world's first application of double-deck sky lobby shuttle elevator. Being the tallest skyscraper in the United States and the third tallest building in the world, surpassed only by the Petronas towers of Malaysia and the Taipei 101, it is 442 m (1,450 feet) tall and has 110 storeys. Sears had to dole out a whopping US$ 2.7 million to the city of Chicago for taking up a part of the street.

Sears Tower (1974), Chicago

Seagram Building (1958), New York

What would be the most critical component in the mega-high-rise buildings?

The mega-high-rise buildings might have a roof-level heliport, a retirement home, child-care facilities, a hospital or medical centre and even a school or college. All these individual components in such buildings would require their own dedicated elevator service. Therefore, stacking would be a vital element in these buildings.

Which is New York's first modern high-rise building?

Built in 1958, and at a height of 160 m (525 feet), 'Seagram Building' is New York's first modern high-rise building. Designed by Mies van der Rohe, the Seagram building epitomises modern construction methods. It is the first building to use a glass covered tower.

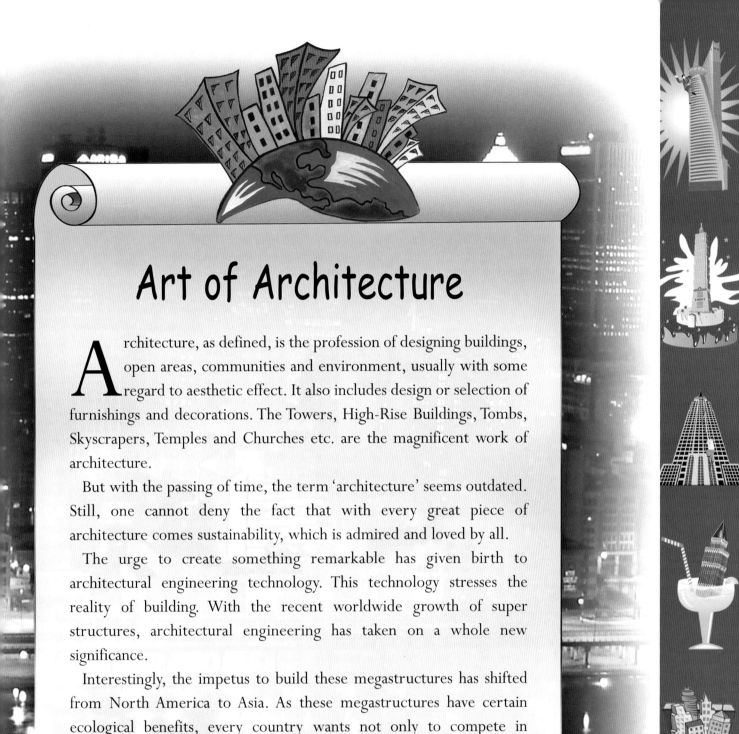

Art of Architecture

Architecture, as defined, is the profession of designing buildings, open areas, communities and environment, usually with some regard to aesthetic effect. It also includes design or selection of furnishings and decorations. The Towers, High-Rise Buildings, Tombs, Skyscrapers, Temples and Churches etc. are the magnificent work of architecture.

But with the passing of time, the term 'architecture' seems outdated. Still, one cannot deny the fact that with every great piece of architecture comes sustainability, which is admired and loved by all.

The urge to create something remarkable has given birth to architectural engineering technology. This technology stresses the reality of building. With the recent worldwide growth of super structures, architectural engineering has taken on a whole new significance.

Interestingly, the impetus to build these megastructures has shifted from North America to Asia. As these megastructures have certain ecological benefits, every country wants not only to compete in technology, but also to create an emblem that is very visible and significant in the skyline.

Art of

Page No.

SKY-HIGH

	Page No.
1. Taipei 101, Taiwan	16
2. PETRONAS Twin Towers, Malaysia	16
3. Empire State Building, US	17
4. First Canadian Place, Canada	18
5. 30 St. Mary Axe, London	18
6. Two International Finance Centre, Hong Kong	19
7. Tuntex Sky Tower, Taiwan	20
8. John Hancock Center, US	20
9. Bank of China Tower, Hong Kong	21
10. Baiyoke Tower II, Thailand	22
11. Emirates Towers, Dubai	22
12. Highcliff and Summit, Hong Kong	23
13. Jin Mao Tower, China	24
14. National Bank of Dubai, Dubai	24
15. Shun Hing Square, China	25
16. Bank of America Tower, US	26
17. Menara Telekom, Malaysia	26
18. Hotel Burj Al Arab, Dubai	27
19. Fountain Place, US	28
20. Westend Straße 1, Germany	28
21. Chelsea Tower, Dubai	29
22. Kingdom Centre, Saudi Arabia	30
23. King Tower, China	30
24. The Tower, Dubai	31

Architecture

		Page No.
25.	Chrysler Building, US	32
26.	Scotia Plaza, Canada	32
27.	Bank of America Center, Houston	33
28.	CITIC Plaza, China	34
29.	TransAmerica Pyramid, US	34
30.	Panglin Plaza, China	35

IN-TOW

31.	Eiffel Tower, France	36
32.	CN Tower, Canada	36
33.	Space Needle Tower, US	37
34.	Oriental Pearl TV Tower, China	38
35.	Big Ben, UK	38
36.	Kuwait Towers, Kuwait	39

WONDERFUL WONDERS

37.	Abu Simbel, Egypt	40
38.	Konark Sun Temple, India	40
39.	Todaiji Temple, Japan	41
40.	Lotus Temple, India	41
41.	St. Basil's Cathedral, Russia	42
42.	Piazza del Duomo, Italy	42
43.	St. Peter's Basilica, Italy	43
44.	Astrodome Houston, US	44
45.	London Eye, UK	44
46.	Taj Mahal, India	45
47.	The Great Wall of China	46

SKY-HIGH

Taipei 101, Taiwan

Taipei 101, located in the city of Taipei and soaring high against the Taiwan Skyline is the world's tallest building.

■ The Taipei 101 building with the height of 510 m (1,672 feet) has dwarfed Sears Tower, Chicago and Petronas Twin Towers, Malaysia.

■ It has 101 storeys above ground and five storeys under ground.

■ The Tower includes a six floor retail mall with shops, restaurants and other attractions.

■ The exterior of the building looks like bamboo segments with eight storeys to each segment.

■ Each segment of the building is created like a sceptre, with ancient coins on the exterior of the 26th floor to give it a chinese look.

PETRONAS Twin Towers, Malaysia

The gleaming Petronas Twin Towers were the largest building in the world until 2004, when they lost this title to Taipei 101

■ The 88-storeyed Twin Towers were designed to symbolise strength and grace.

■ A two-storey tall sky bridge links the two towers at the 41st and 42nd storeys.

■ Twin Towers are a striking glass and steel combination with floor plans based on an eight-pointed star.

■ Designed by Cesar Pelli, Petronas Twin Towers are the world's first application of double-deck sky lobby shuttles.

■ The Towers house the headquarters of Petronas, the National Petroleum Company of Malaysia.

Empire State Building, US

The Empire State Building was declared as one of the modern Seven Wonders of the World.

■ Prominent on many postcards, Empire State Building is probably New York's best known landmark.

■ Described as 'the most valuable building in American Broadcasting', the building has 6,500 windows, 73 elevators and 1,860 steps to the top floor.

■ The 381 m (1,250 feet) tall building has been featured in over 90 movies.

■ The top of the building has been visited by over 100 million people.

■ It remained the tallest building in the world for many years, until the completion of the first tower of the World Trade Center, Lower Manhattan in 1972.

■ The Building takes its name from the nickname of the New York State.

■ In 1945, an Army Aircorps B-25 bomber plane crashed into the 79th floor of the building in dense fog. Fourteen people died and the building incurred a loss of US$ 1 million.

For many years, Empire State Building was known as Empty State Building as the owners simply could not find tenants.

Fact File

Building Name	Height (in feet)	No. of Storeys	Date of Completion
Taipei 101	1,672	106	2004
Petronas Tower	1,483	88	1998
Empire State Building	1,250	102	1931

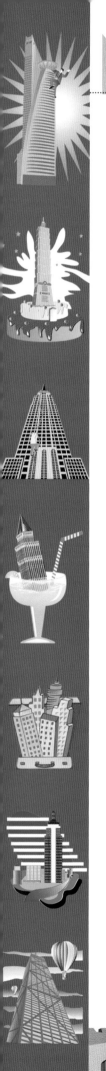

SKY-HIGH

First Canadian Place, Canada

First Canadian Place, Canada's tallest skyscraper, has remained unchallenged as the tallest office building in Canada since it was constructed in 1975.

■ It is an impressive 72-storeyed office, banking and shopping complex.

■ With the highest rooftop in Canada, it serves as a prime communication site.

■ 298 m (977 feet) high, First Canadian Place is home to the Toronto headquarters of 'The Bank of Montreal'.

■ The gracious building is noted for its white stone finish.

■ Equipped with advanced technology, the building has 29 double-decker passenger elevators.

30 St. Mary Axe, London

St. Mary Axe is London's first environment sustainable tall building.

■ The windows of this building are designed to allow as abundance of fresh air and light inside the building.

■ Developed by Swiss Re and designed by architects Foster and Partners, this building was completed in 2003.

■ The bottom of this 41-storeyed building is circular, which tapers gradually to the top.

■ The shape of the building makes the tower appear slimmer than a rectilinear building of the same size.

■ The retail space is given at the ground level which opens onto a landscaped plaza.

Two International Finance Centre, Hong Kong

Designed by Cesar Pelli, Two International Finance Centre is Hong Kong's tallest building.

- It is a set of two towers International Finance Centre I and International Finance Centre II.

- Completed in 1998, International Finance Centre I has 88 storeys and 22 trading floors.

- Completed in 2003, International Finance Centre II has 39 storeys and four trading floors.

- It has advanced telecommunications and a nearly column-free floor plan.

- This High-Rise is designed for offices of financial companies.

Two International Finance Centre Building has featured in the Hollywood movie Tomb Raider: The Cradle of Life.

Fact File

Building Name	Height (in feet)	No. of Storeys	Date of Completion
First Canadian Place	977	72	1975
30 St. Mary Axe	590	41	2003
IFC-1	590	39	1998
IFC-2	1,378	88	2003

SKY-HIGH

Tuntex Sky Tower, Taiwan

The Tuntex Sky Tower dons the mantle of the third tallest building in Asia

■ The Tower has an unusual 'prong' design with two separate 35-floor lower towers merging into a single central tower rising to a spire.

■ Tuntex Sky Tower is a skyscraper in Kaohsiung, Taiwan.

■ The 85-storeyed Tower is designed by C.Y. Lee and Partners, and Hellmuth.

■ It has the highest hotel rooms in Taiwan and the second highest hotel rooms in the world.

■ Tuntex Sky Tower replaced Chang-Gu World Trade Center as the tallest building in Kaohsiung.

John Hancock Center, US

John Hancock Center locally known as 'Big John' has a remarkable design with the huge X-braces serving both a structural and a visual purpose.

■ The 344 m (1,128 feet) multi-use building is known for its distinctive architecture and presence on the Chicago skyline.

■ A 100-storeyed building, completed in 1969, it is a much sought after place by both large and small office tenants.

■ The multi-functional building includes 48 storeys of apartments, and 29 storeys of offices, shops, a hotel, a swimming pool, an ice-rink, restaurant, radio and television facilities.

Bank of China Tower, Hong Kong

A striking hard-edged asymmetrical structure featuring triangular prisms that create changing vistas on viewing it from different sides.

■ Symbolic of strength, vitality, growth and enterprise, the Bank of China Tower is 369 m (1,210 feet) high.

■ No longer the tallest building in Hong Kong, the 72-storeyed tower remains Hong Kong's most readily identifiable structure.

■ With a harmonious blend of modern architecture and traditional Chinese design, the building is designed by Architect I.M. Pei and Partners.

■ With blue glass and white framing, the tower rises majestically from its central location.

I.M. Pei's original plans included an X-shaped cross-brace. He had to drop it, because in China the X-shape is considered to be a symbol of death.

Fact File

Building Name	Height (in feet)	No. of Storeys	Date of Completion
Tuntex Sky Tower	1,140	85	1997
John Hancock Center	1,128	100	1969
Bank of China Tower	1,210	72	1990

SKY-HIGH

Baiyoke Tower II, Thailand

Baiyoke Tower II is unique with its Sky Walk on the 77th floor, which is Thailand's only open-air, 360 degree revolving roof-deck.

■ Commonly known as Baiyoke Sky Hotel, it was one of the first high-rise buildings in Bangkok which utilised high strength concrete for construction.

■ The Tower, Thailand's tallest and Bangkok's most scenic hotel, rises 85 storeys above the Bangkok skyline.

■ Designed by Plan Architects Company, the hotel is situated between the 22nd and 74th floor, having 673 guest-rooms.

■ The circular top of the building is golden—symbolising wealth.

■ Located in the heart of city, the hotel is surrounded by a bustling market and various entertainment attractions.

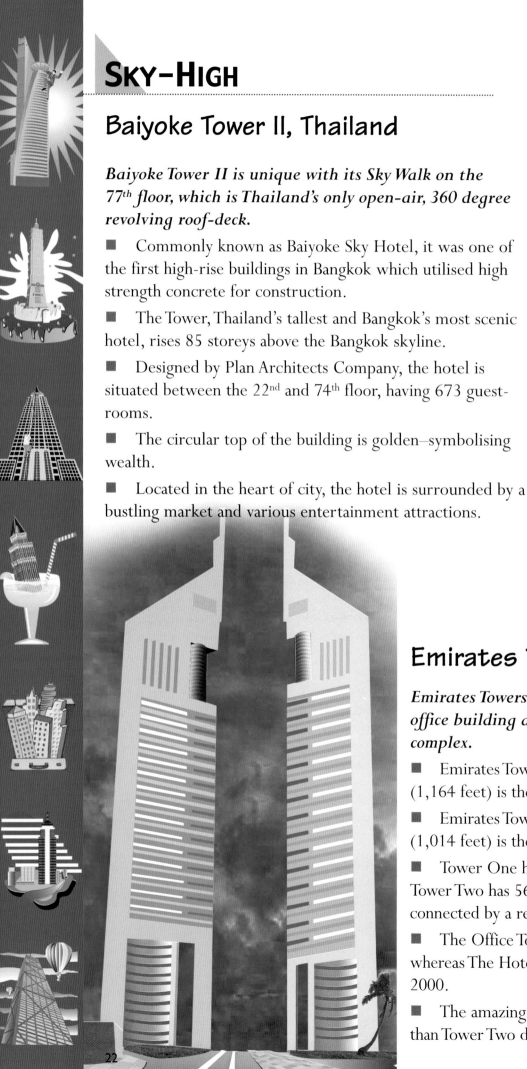

Emirates Towers, Dubai

Emirates Towers is an alliance between an office building and a hotel—creating a huge complex.

■ Emirates Tower One at a height of 355 m (1,164 feet) is the Emirates Office Tower.

■ Emirates Tower Two at a height of 309 m (1,014 feet) is the Emirates Hotel Tower.

■ Tower One has 54 floors whereas the Tower Two has 56 floors, both the towers are connected by a retail boulevard.

■ The Office Tower was completed in 1999 whereas The Hotel Tower was completed in 2000.

■ The amazing fact is that Tower One is taller than Tower Two despite having two less floors.

Highcliff and Summit, Hong Kong

These Towers are known for having the most expensive residential apartments.

■ Highcliff and Summit are twin towers which are the latest additions to the luxury property market in Hong Kong.

■ Highcliff, a 72-storeyed, 252 m (828 feet) high deluxe apartment located on the hillsides of Hong Kong Island was completed in 2003.

■ Summit, a 65-storeyed, 220 m (722 feet) high deluxe apartment was completed in 2001.

■ Designed by Dennis Lau and Ng Chun Man Architects and Engineers (HK) Ltd., the buildings allow two units per floor.

■ Each typical unit has a double-height living room connected to two floors.

Highcliff and Summit are the tallest structures in the world to have only residential apartments.

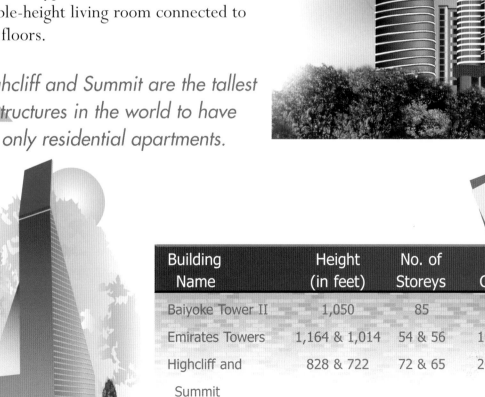

Fact File

Building Name	Height (in feet)	No. of Storeys	Date of Completion
Baiyoke Tower II	1,050	85	1997
Emirates Towers	1,164 & 1,014	54 & 56	1999 & 2000
Highcliff and Summit	828 & 722	72 & 65	2003 & 2001

SKY-HIGH

Jin Mao Tower, China

Representing a triumph of modern engineering and architectural theory, Jin Mao Tower, Shangai is the third tallest tower on earth.

- Jin Mao, stands for wealth and prosperity.
- Completed in 1999, this commercial office tower graces the Shanghai skyline and it also holds the title of 'The World's Tallest Hotel Rooms.'
- The 88-storeyed Tower is a synthesis of traditional Chinese architectural style with modern advanced technologies.
- The Tower's glass screen wall enhances its beauty at night, after being illuminated by neon lights.

National Bank of Dubai, Dubai

The National Bank of Dubai has kept pace with every stage of Dubai's development.

- With total dedication to sound banking practices, The National Bank has formed a very conservative image for itself.
- Its imposing new headquarters, depicts a ship in full sail.
- The design and layout of the new creek side, 20-storeyed headquarters building is inspired by the philosophy of the bank.

Shun Hing Square, China

The Shun Hing Square is the tallest steel building at Shenzhen in China

■ 384 m (1,260 feet) high, the Tower is a thin slab with rounded corners clad in glass.

■ Without its spires, the building's height is 325 m (1,066 feet).

■ The 69-storeyed building provides offices, apartments, a car park and shopping arcade complex.

■ Completed in 1996 at a very fast pace, Shun Hing Square has an observation floor called 'Meridian View Centre' at the 69th floor.

■ The shopping arcade is a huge five-storeyed mall with four sets of escalators, five passenger lifts and two service lifts.

■ Designed by K.Y. Cheung Design Associates, it has 330 high class residential flats and an office space of 144,200 m² (1,552,155 sq. feet).

The Shun Hing Square is the tallest Steel Building in China.

Fact File

Building Name	Height (in feet)	No. of Storeys	Date of Completion
Jin Mao Tower	1,380	88	1999
National Bank of Dubai	410	20	1998
Shun Hing Square	1,260	69	1996

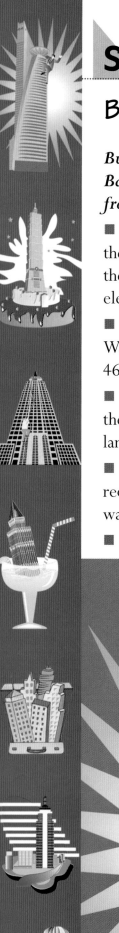

Sky-High

Bank of America Tower, US

Built in the financial centre of Seattle, the Bank of America Tower's striking beauty comes from its simple black glass blocks.

■ Standing tall at a massive 304 m (997 feet), the Tower was made all the more graceful through the use of three sweeping arcs of multiple elevations.

■ Designed by Chester L. Lindsay Architects of Washington, the Tower is the proud possessor of 46 elevators and six express elevators.

■ Originally planned to be 306 m (1,005 feet), the height was reduced by eight feet to facilitate the landing of planes into Sea-Tac airport.

■ The developers invented a novel way of reducing height. The ceiling height of each floor was reduced by 15 cm (6 inches).

■ The building has both office and retail space.

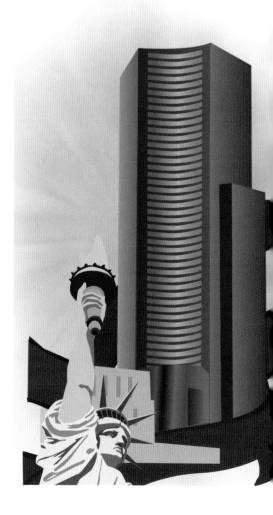

Menara Telekom, Malaysia

Standing tall at 310 m (1,017 feet), Menara Telekom, Kuala Lumpur is the fifth tallest telecommunication tower in the world.

■ Built in 2003 to enhance the quality of telecommunication and clarity in broadcasting, the tower symbolises a sprout of bamboo shooting up from the earth.

■ Designed by Hijjas Kasturi and Associates, the 55-storeyed Tower has been given a soft touch by beautiful terrace gardens after every three floors.

■ The main lobby on the upper ground floor has glass domes which glow like crystal balls.

■ In constructing the Tower, the builders took special care to construct a retaining wall around a 100-year-old Julutong Tree.

Hotel Burj Al Arab, Dubai

The Burj Al Arab means 'The Arabian Tower' in Arabic.

■ The Burj Al Arab, a luxury hotel in Dubai, is built on a tiny man-made island, away from the beach with foundation pillars reaching underneath the sea-bed.

■ Looking like a giant sail, the huge structure looks slightly shorter due to an optical illusion.

■ Completed in 1999, at a height of 321 m (1,053 feet), the hotel is placed in such a way that its shadow does not cover the beach.

■ Its Teflon-coated exterior is brilliant white during a sunny day, but takes on an entirely different hue at night.

■ The top of the building is shaped to be used as a helipad.

■ Contrary to popular belief, the Burj Al Arab is not a seven-star, but only a five-star deluxe hotel.

The cost of building the hotel was so high that it must be booked for 400 years for it to make a profit.

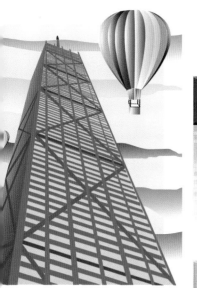

Fact File

Building Name	Height (in feet)	No. of Storeys	Date of Completion
Bank of America Tower	997	76	1985
Menara Telekom	1,017	55	2001
Hotel Burj Al Arab	1,053	60	1999

SKY-HIGH

Fountain Place, US

Looking at its ten-sided exterior of vertical and angled walls, it never appears the same from any given angle.

■ Fountain Place, a unique 62-storeyed skyscraper whose base is square in shape, looks like a glittering glass prism from far away.

■ At a height of 220 m (720 feet), it is the fifth tallest building in Dallas.

■ Designed by I.M. Pei and Partners, half of the building has been left for a water garden and fountain plaza. The plaza has over 172 fountains and waterfalls under shady cypress trees.

■ For this superior architecture, the architects were recognised with an Honour Award from the American Institute of Architects in 1990.

Westend Straße 1, Germany

This 53-storeyed building used impressive innovations such as a steel cornice-fan, on its roof, which is heated in winter to prevent icing.

■ Westend Straße 1 is located along the famous Mainzer Landstrasse in Frankfurt, Germany.

■ It was completed in 1993.

■ Westend Straße 1 stands between a commercial complex and a residential area.

■ The Building is made of glass on one side and stone on the other.

■ In tune with Frankfurt's permissible height for tall buildings until 1989, Westend Straße's height was confined to 150 m (492 feet).

Chelsea Tower, Dubai

The most striking feature of the building design is the white diagonal spine that stretches from the ground to its apex.

■ At a height of 230 m (754 feet), the two sides of the spine join to form a perfect square opening.

■ At the centre of this square opening hangs a 40 m (131 feet) high needle which stretches the overall height of the tower to 250 m (820 feet).

■ With 282 apartments, the building was completed in 2005.

■ The roof of the car park building behind the tower accommodates a 25 m (82 feet) long swimming pool, gymnasium and squash courts.

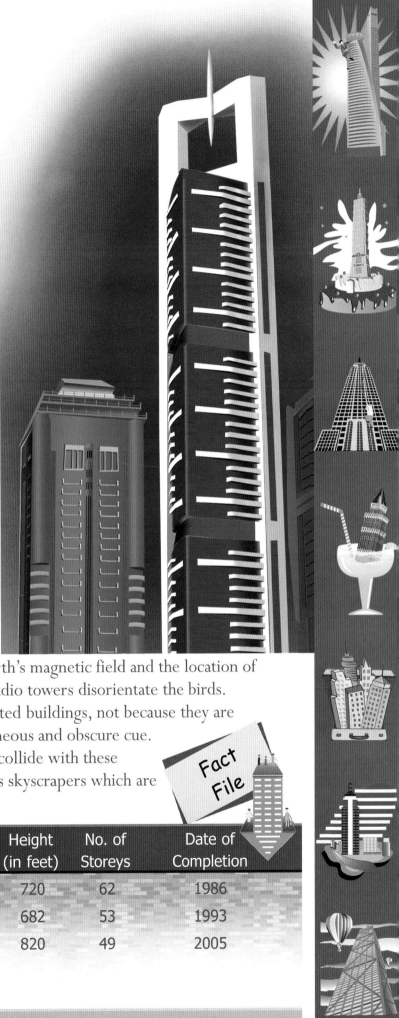

Skyscrapers and Birds

Birds use a variety of different cues to navigate their migration route, including the pattern of the stars, topographic features, the Earth's magnetic field and the location of the setting Sun. The light's of tall buildings and radio towers disorientate the birds. These confused birds will then circle the illuminated buildings, not because they are attracted, but because they are following an erroneous and obscure cue. Eventually many of these birds may collide with these skyscrapers specially with glass skyscrapers which are brilliantly lit at night.

Fact File

Building Name	Height (in feet)	No. of Storeys	Date of Completion
Fountain Place	720	62	1986
Westend Straße 1	682	53	1993
Chelsea Tower	820	49	2005

SKY-HIGH

Kingdom Centre, Saudi Arabia

Inspired by the design of a necklace, the Kingdom Centre is a perfect example of design and functionality.

■ Kingdom Centre in Riyadh is the tallest skyscraper in Saudi Arabia.

■ The Tower's symmetry is in accordance with the traditions of Islamic art with a range of geometric forms.

■ The 41-storeyed Centre includes a hotel, state-of-the-art apartments besides the shopping mall.

■ The Centre is owned by Prince Alwaleed Bin Talal of the Saudi Royal Family.

■ The four entrances of the building help in differentiating its uses.

King Tower, China

The King Tower basked in the glory of being the tallest building of China for few months till it was dwarfed by Shun Hing Square.

■ Designed by Tao Ho architects, the King Tower was completed in 1996.

■ It is located on the left of CAAC Pudong Tower in the city of Shanghai.

■ A high-rise building, it soars to a height of 212 m (696 feet).

■ Shaped like a rocket, it has 38 storeys.

The Tower, Dubai

The Tower is crowned with a pyramid shape aluminium and glass spire which enhances its slender figure.

■ The Tower's outer façade is covered with glass and marked by slender steel strips which cross over to form a pointed arch motif with an Arabian flavour.

■ It was designed by architects Khatib and Alami of Lebanon.

■ Opened in April 2002, the building rises 243 m (796 feet) high into the air.

■ The Tower accommodates both offices and apartments.

■ The 372 apartments were designed to permit optimal distribution of space, for luxury and comfort.

The Tower, Dubai was constructed at a frantic pace. Each storey took only three days to be built. This was made possible by using pre-fabricated concrete, steel and glass material.

Fact File

Building Name	Height (in feet)	No. of Storeys	Date of Completion
Kingdom Centre	992	41	2002
CAAC Pudong Tower	696	38	2001
The Tower	796	54	2002

LONDON

SKY-HIGH

Chrysler Building, US

The 77-storeyed building is one of the first large buildings to use metal extensively on the exterior.

■ Constructing the highest building in the world was a status symbol for Walter Chrysler, an automobile tycoon.

■ With a height of 320 m (1,048 feet), the Chrysler Building was one of the most decorated office buildings in the world.

■ Completed in 1930, it is one of the last skyscrapers in the Art Deco style.

■ Designed by William Van Alen, it enjoyed a brief stint of being the tallest building until the Empire State Building dwarfed it.

■ The building's interior and decorative scheme is largely geometric.

Scotia Plaza, Canada

Scotia Plaza, a 68-storeyed building, wrapped in napoleonic granite, catches the eye from a distance.

■ The unique aspect of the building is a 40 m (130 feet) high atrium called the 'Circle of the Provinces.'

■ Designed by WZMH Architects, Scotia Plaza is made up of three integrated buildings.

■ At a height of 275 m (902 feet), Scotia Plaza is Toronto's second tallest building.

■ Full height windows supply an abundance of natural light in each floor's 22 corner offices.

■ Besides, it incorporates an advanced air handling system to ensure fresh air inside.

Bank of America Center, Houston

Built in 1983, Bank of America Center is Houston's only attempt at a classic 1920's-style skyscraper.

■ It is an example of what happens when you crossbreed skyscrapers with old houses.

■ At the height of 238 m (780 feet), Bank of America Center is dark pink in appearance being clad in red Swedish granite.

■ The first section is 21 storeys tall, while the whole building reaches a height of 56 storeys.

■ The building stands out from other buildings in the skyline which are blue, black and white.

■ The skyscraper envelopes the old two-storeyed Western Union building inside this hall.

■ The building succeeds in taking something from the outside world and adapting it to meet local sensibilities.

■ The skyscraper has changed its name three times since its completion. Originally named Republic Center, it was later renamed Nations Bank Center and is now called the Bank of America Center.

Bank of America Building won honours as Regional Building of the Year from the Building Owners and Managers Association.

Fact File

Building Name	Height (in feet)	No. of Storeys	Date of Completion
Chrysler Building	1,048	77	1930
Scotia Plaza	902	68	1988
Bank of America Center	780	56	1983

SKY-HIGH

CITIC Plaza, China

Located in the hub of commercial activity, the 80-storeyed CITIC Plaza is the business address of many international companies.

■ CITIC Plaza, located in Tianhe District of Guangzhou city is the tallest building of Guangzhou.

■ At the height of 391 m (1,283 feet), the main tower is flanked by two subordinate buildings of 38 storeys, together with a five-storeyed apron building.

■ The Subordinate Towers are used as offices and apartments.

■ Completed in 1997, the plaza has a shopping arcade as well.

■ The arcade has a gorgeous lobby 21.3 m (70 feet) in height with a round glass ceiling.

TransAmerica Pyramid, US

Since its completion in 1972, the TransAmerica Pyramid has become one of the most recognised buildings in the United States.

■ The 260 m (853 feet) high office tower is topped by a 65 m (212 feet) needle-shaped spire.

■ The pyramid shape of this 48-storeyed office tower dominates the San Francisco skyline and is visible from most parts of the town.

■ Designed by William Pereira and Associates, the pyramid is flanked by a set of structures that look like wings.

■ The eastern wing is an elevator shaft whereas the western wing has a stairwell.

■ Its tapered lines allow more sunlight and air to penetrate into the street level.

Panglin Plaza, China

The Sky Paradise, a revolving restaurant on the 50th floor is the most prominent feature of the building from where one can enjoy panoramic views of both Shenzhen and Hong Kong.

- Panglin Plaza is an elegant five-star hotel located right in the heart of Shenzhen's Lower commercial district.

- The Apollo 57 sightseeing tower on 56th–57th floor is another striking aspect of the 240 m (787 feet) high building.

- The hotel has stylish bars, restaurants, a ballroom, 382 standard rooms and suites, a conference hall and many recreational facilities.

- Completed in 1999, Panglin Plaza stands for elegance and comfort.

New Safety Measures

The collapse of the World Trade Center has added a new dimension to the concept of safety of buildings. In Asia, Herculean Towers with state-of-the-art safety features have already arrived.

Skyscrapers in Asia have more safety features. The Shanghai World Financial Centre has a reinforced concrete core with a dedicated fire lift and refuge floors at every 15 levels. These are designed to be totally fire proof so that they can harbour people in the middle of an evacuation.

Fact File

Building Name	Height (in feet)	No. of Storeys	Date of Completion
CITIC Plaza	1,283	80	1997
TransAmerica Pyramid	853	48	1972
Panglin Plaza	787	57	1999

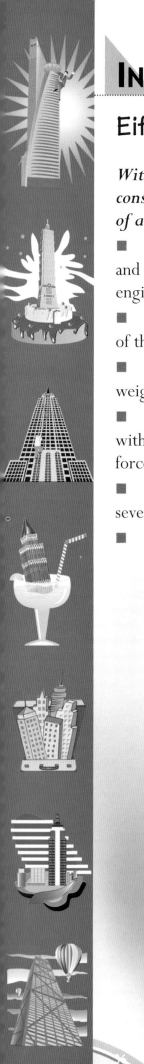

IN-TOW

Eiffel Tower, France

With lace-like iron detailing, it is widely considered to be one of the most striking pieces of architecture in the world.

■ Eiffel Tower is the most famous landmark, and symbol of Paris, named after its designer, engineer Gustave Eiffel.

■ It was built in 1889, to celebrate the centenary of the French revolution.

■ Standing tall at 324 m (1,063 feet), the total weight of the tower is 10,100 metric tons.

■ A light, airy but strong structure was erected within two years with the help of a small labour force.

■ Having 1,665 steps, the tower is painted every seven years to protect it from rust.

■ It is used as a transmission tower for FM and TV.

CN Tower, Canada

The CN Tower was classified as one of the seven wonders of the modern world by the American Society of Civil Engineers.

■ Completed in 1976, the CN Tower was built for the Canadian National Railway.

■ 553 m (1,815 feet) high, the Tower was originally designed as a radio and television transmitting antenna.

■ Built by Canadian National Railway to demonstrate the strength of Canadian industry, CN Tower soon found it was far more lucrative as a tourist attraction.

■ The Tower has a Glass Floor, a Horizons café and a Restaurant at three different decks which collectively are known as the Sky Pod.

Space Needle Tower, US

The Space Needle Tower was once bathed by over 200 floodlights, hence it was called the Northern Light Tower.

- It is 184 m (605 feet) high.
- The Space Needle Tower is the Pacific Northwest's most recognisable landmark and is the symbol of Seattle, Washington.
- It was completed in 1961 at the cost of US$ 4.5 million.
- It is built to withstand winds upto 320 km/h (199 mph) and earthquakes upto 9.1 on Richter Scale. It has 25 lightning rods on the roof to withstand lighting strikes.
- A powerful beam of light called the skybeam is unveiled from the top of the Space Needle to honour national holidays and special occasions.
- The unique architecture of the tower is designed by Edward Carlson and John Graham.
- The top dome of the building houses the observation deck and restaurants.

During World War II, when Adolf Hitler visited German-occupied Paris, the Parisians cut the wire of the lift cables to the Eiffel Tower so that Adolf Hitler would have a laborious journey to the top via the staircase. Hitler however, chose to remain on the ground.

IN-Tow

Oriental Pearl TV Tower, China

The Tower is the world's third tallest TV and radio tower after CN Tower in Toronto and Moscow TV Tower.

■ Built in 1994, the Tower is an important landmark and a fascination to tourists.

■ It serves the Shanghai area with more than nine television channels and over 10 FM radio channels.

■ The Tower has a central support structure, with three columns, each 9 m (30 feet) in diameter. Supplementing these at the base are three more braces, each 7 m (23 feet) in diameter plunged into the ground.

■ Designed by Jia Huan Cheng, the design of the building is based on a Tan dynasty poem about the haunting sound made by a flute.

Big Ben, UK

Big Ben is often used as a symbol for London in tourist guides.

■ Designed by E.B. Denison, built by E.J. Dent, and later by F. Dent, the clock has hands 2.7 m (9 feet) and 4.3 m (14 feet) long respectively.

■ Cast by George Mears of White Chapel and weighing more than 13 tons, the bell was dragged to the tower by 16 horses.

■ The name Big Ben was applied only to the bell, but it eventually came to indicate the clock itself.

Kuwait Towers, Kuwait

The Kuwait Towers hold 4,500 cubic metres of water, which is used for the consumption of the entire population of the city of Kuwait.

■ Designed by Sune Lindström and Malene Björn of Sweden, it fuses traditional Arabic with modern architecture, reflecting the country's cultural heritage.

■ 140 m (459 feet) tall, the first tower supports a water-holding sphere.

■ 180 m (590 feet) tall, the second tower has a restaurant and a cafeteria.

■ The third Tower has no spheres, but has 96 concealed spotlights for lighting.

■ The tallest tower has a restaurant, a snack bar, a café, and a sphere which rotates once in every 30 minutes providing panoramic view of the Kuwait City and the Arabian Gulf.

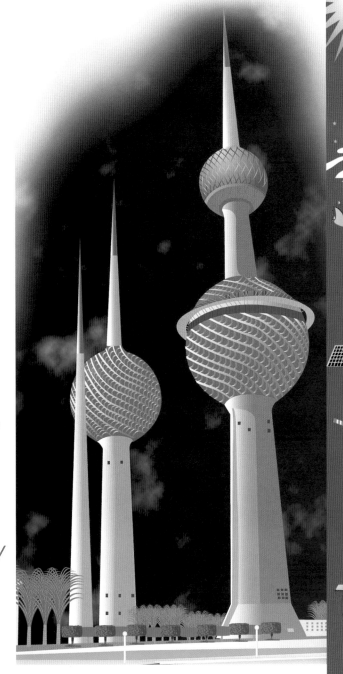

Big Ben is a focus of New Year celebrations in the UK, with radio and TV stations tuning to its chimes to welcome the official start of the New Year.

One of the most magnificent edifices in Kuwait, the Kuwait Towers renders a distinct architectural expression that combines utility with aesthetics.

WONDERFUL WONDERS

Abu Simbel, Egypt

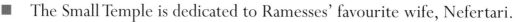

The alignment of the temple Abu Simbel is such that twice a year the Sun's rays reach into the innermost sanctuary to illuminate the temple.

■ Abu Simbel is a set of two temples near the border of Egypt with Sudan.

■ The Great Temple is dedicated to Ramesses II whose statue is seated with three other Gods.

■ The Small Temple is dedicated to Ramesses' favourite wife, Nefertari.

■ The Temple was cut out of the sandstone cliffs above the Nile River.

■ Construction of the Aswan High Dam threatened the temples with submersion under the rising waters of the Lake Nassar, and it led to the demolition of both the temples and the reconstruction of them 61 m (200 feet) above the original site.

Konark Sun Temple, India

Conceived as a chariot of the Sun God, the temple has three images of the Sun God, which are positioned to catch the rays of sun at dawn, noon and sunset.

■ Konark Sun Temple is located in the state of Orissa, near the sacred city of Puri.

■ Dedicated to the Sun God, it is a masterpiece of Orissa's medieval architecture

■ Built in the 13th century by King Narasimha, the entire temple has been conceived as a chariot of the Sun God with 24 wheels, each with a set of spokes and elaborate carvings.

■ The shadows formed by the spokes can give the precise time of the day.

■ The temple has been declared as a world heritage site by UNESCO.

Todaiji Temple, Japan

48 m (157 feet) high, constructed with wood, the temple is considered to be the largest wooden building in the world.

▦ Todaiji, a temple complex in the city of Nara, is one of the oldest Buddhist temples in Japan.

▦ The temple houses a 15 m (49 feet) high mammoth statue of Lord Buddha, Diabutsu, cast in gilded bronze.

▦ The base of the statue that remains today dates back to the 8th century, while the upper portion was largely recast in the second half of the 12th century.

▦ The original Shosoin inside the temple serves as the repository for the temple treasure.

Lotus Temple, India

The traditional concept has been given a modern design in the construction of Bahai temple, more popularly known as the Lotus Temple.

▦ Right in the heart of India's capital Delhi, the East and West meet creating one of the finest pieces of architecture in modern times.

▦ Shaped like a huge half opened lotus flower, the temple is designed by Faviborz Subha, a Canadian architect of Iranian origin.

▦ The complex structure of the temple consists of three ranks of nine petals each, rising from a podium.

▦ The temple has nine entrances as number 'Nine' holds special significance in the Bahai faith.

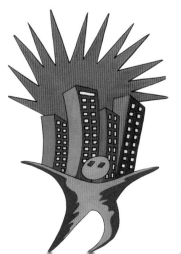

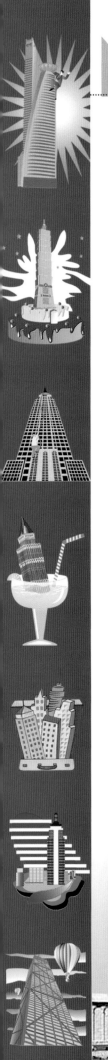

WONDERFUL WONDERS

St. Basil's Cathedral, Russia

There is a legend that the Tzar ordered the architect of the Church to be blinded so that he could never create its like again.

■ St. Basil's Church, on the edge of Red Square, Moscow is one of the oldest as well as one of the most beautiful churches in the world.

■ It was built between 1556 and 1561 under the reign of the Russian Tzar nicknamed 'Ivan the terrible.'

■ Though the exterior of the Church is flamboyant, the interior is sober.

■ St. Basil's has a delightful array of swirling colours and red brick towers.

■ Its design is comprised of nine individual chapels, each topped with a unique onion dome. The eight towers are positioned around a ninth spire, forming an eight-point star. The number eight carries great religious significance.

Piazza del Duomo, Italy

Standing in a large green expanse, Piazza del Duomo houses a group of monuments known all over the world.

■ These four masterpieces of medieval architecture – the cathedral, baptistry, the campanile and the cemetery — had a great influence on monumental art in Italy from the 11th–14th century.

■ The Cathedral, built in 1418, has been the religious and cultural centre of the city.

■ The Baptistry, built between the 5th and 9th centuries, was believed to have originated as a Roman temple.

■ The Campanile, designed by Giotto, has a pink, green and white marble exterior.

■ Most of the Piazza del Duomo's art resides in a modern-looking museum, Museo dell 'Opera del Duomo'.

St. Peter's Basilica, Italy

Where St. Peter's Basilica stands now was once a chariot racing stadium, built in the time of the Emperors Caligula, Claudius and Nero.

■ St. Peter, who was persecuted by Nero, was buried in the nearest cemetery, just right of the stadium.

■ Many great artists were involved in the construction and decoration of this Basilica above the tomb of St. Peter.

■ The tomb of St. Peter is still there underneath the front of the Papal Altar and about 6 m (20 feet) below the floor level of the Basilica.

■ The design of the Basilica incorporates a sun dial, a calendar and the welcoming arms of God's embrace.

■ From the balcony above the central door, the Pope comes to address the world after his election and on the feasts of Christmas and Easter.

■ The space is large enough to hold about 90,000 people.

WONDERFUL WONDERS

Astrodome Houston, US

It is the first astrodome to have a plastic roof over the playing field.

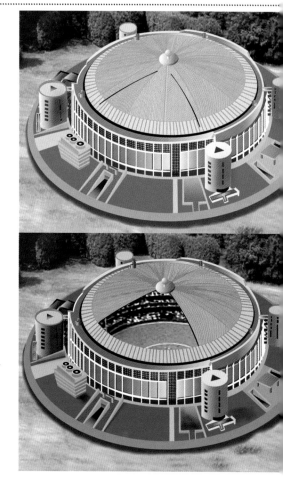

■ Originally known as the Harris County Domed Stadium, the stadium opened in 1965.

■ The Astrodome Houston became home to the University of Houston's football team in 1965.

■ Due to the plastic roof, not enough sunlight was reaching the playing surface, which resulted in the death of natural grass. A green surface of nylon grass called Astroturf was introduced instead.

■ The Astrodome boasts of a seating capacity of 60,000 spectators, 53 sky boxes and a scoreboard.

■ To illuminate the field requires more electricity than is used by the entire city.

■ A car park built on a 260-acre tract could accommodate around 30,000 cars.

London Eye, UK

Looking like a gigantic spoked bicycle wheel, it is the largest observation wheel in the world and is also known as Millennium Wheel.

■ Designed by, David Marks and Julia Barfield, the wheel carries 32 sealed air-conditioned passenger capsules attached to its external circumference.

■ Its total weight is 1,700 tonnes and height is 135 m (443 feet).

■ It rotates at a rate of 0.26 m (0.85 feet) per second so that a complete revolution takes about 30 minutes to complete.

■ As it moves slowly one can easily alight and later board it to get a panoramic view of landmarks and buildings.

■ The wheel was constructed in sections, which were floated up the river Thames on barges and assembled flat on pontoons, before being raised into upright positions by cranes.

■ It was lifted at a rate of about 2 degrees per hour until it reached 65 degrees, where it remained for a week while engineers planned for the next phase of the lift.

Taj Mahal, India

Taj Mahal, regarded as one of the eight wonders of the world, is sheer poetry in white marble, an epitome of love.

■ A fine blend of Indian, Persian, and Islamic styles, it was built by the Mughal Emperor Shah Jahan to immortalise his wife, Mumtaz Mahal.

■ The complex, a unified entity, has five principal elements – main gateway, garden, mosque, jawab (a building mirroring the mosque), and mausoleum (including its four minarets).

■ Its architectural beauty is beyond description, particularly at dawn and at sunset.

■ The entire mausoleum is decorated with inlaids design of flowers and calligraphy using precious gems.

■ The mausoleum reflects various hues according to the intensity of the sun or moonlight.

■ It has four almost identical façades, each with a wide central arch with slanted corners incorporating smaller arches. The majestic central dome reaches to a height of 73 m (240 feet).

■ It took more than 20,000 people and 22 years to build this magnificent structure.

WONDERFUL WONDERS

The Great Wall of China

Renovated from time to time, the Great Wall we see today is mostly from the Ming Dynasty.

- Like a gigantic dragon, the Great Wall winds up and down stretching approximately 6,700 km (4,163 miles) from east to west of China.

- With a history of more than 2,000 years, it is one of the most appealing attractions all around the world owing to its architectural grandeur and historical significance.

- It is believed to have originated as a military fortification, guarding against invasion by tribes on the borders during the earlier Zhou Dynasty.

- The materials used were whatever could be found nearby — clay, stone, willow branches, reeds and sand.

- The Great Wall, reputed as one of the seven construction wonders in the world, was enlisted in the World Heritage by UNESCO in 1987.

GLOSSARY

Aesthetic: Appreciating beauty and beautiful things; pleasing to look at; artistic; tasteful.

Arcade: An arched or covered passageway, usually with shops on each side.

Astrodome: A transparent dome on top of the fuselage of an aircraft, through which observations are made for celestial navigation.

Bask: Sit or lie enjoying warmth.

Cathedral: A very large and important church which has a bishop in charge of it.

Dwarfed: Making something appear small in comparison with something else.

Epitome: Representative of a great quality.

Façade: The front of a building, an imposing or decorative one.

Grandeur: The quality of being impressive and often elegant.

Iconic: Having characteristics of an icon.

Igloo: A dome-shaped structure made from blocks of ice.

Impetus: Something that causes and encourages a given response.

Masonry: Constructions using stone and mortar.

Meridian: Imaginary circle on the earth's surface passing through North and South poles.

Panoramic: An unobstructed and wide view of an extensive area in all directions.

Papal: Papal is used to describe anythings related to the Pope.

Pontoon: A floating structure such as a flat-bottom boat.

Prism: A transparent solid body, having a triangular base, used for dispersing light into a spectrum.

Prong: Each of the two or more long pointed parts of a fork.

Repository: A place which can be used for storage.

Sceptre: Staff or rod carried by a ruler as a symbol of royal power.

Spire: A tall cone-shaped structure on the top of a building such as a church.

Subterranean: Underground; under the earth's surface.

Suite: A connected series of rooms to be used together.

Tepee: Cone-shaped tent, made of skins or bark on a frame of poles, used by American–Indians.

Vistas: Long series of scenes, events, etc. that one can look back on or forward to.

INDEX

A

Abu Simbel, Egypt **40**

Astrodome Houston, US **44**

B

Baiyoke Tower II, Thailand **22**

Bank of America Center, Houston **33**

Bank of America Tower, US **26**

Bank of China Tower, Hong Kong **21**

Big Ben, UK **38**

C

Chelsea Tower, Dubai **29**

Chrysler Building, US **32**

CITIC Plaza, China **34**

CN Tower, Canada **36**

Columbus Memorial Building, US **8**

E

Eiffel Tower, France **36**

Emirates Towers, Dubai **22**

Empire State Building, US **17**

F

First Canadian Place, Canada **18**

Fountain Place, US **28**

H

Highcliff and Summit, Hong Kong **23**

Home Insurance Office Building, US **7**

Hotel Burj Al Arab, Dubai **27**

J

Jin Mao Tower, China **24**

John Hancock Center, US **20**

K

King Tower, China **30**

Kingdom Centre, Saudi Arabia **30**

Konark Sun Temple, India **40**

Kuwait Towers, Kuwait **39**

L

London Eye, UK **44**

Lotus Temple, India **41**

Ludington Building, US **8**

M

Masonic Temple, US **10**

Menara Telekom, Malaysia **26**

N

National Bank of Dubai, Dubai **24**

O

Oriental Pearl TV Tower, China **38**

P

Panglin Plaza, China **35**

PETRONAS Twin Towers, Malaysia **16**

Piazza del Duomo, Italy **42**

S

Scotia Plaza, Canada **32**

Seagram Building, US **12**

Sears Tower, US **12**

Shun Hing Square, China **25**

Singer Building, US **11**

Space Needle Tower, US **37**

St. Basil's Cathedral, Russia **42**

St. Peter's Basilica, Italy **43**

T

Taipei 101, Taiwan **16**

Taj Mahal, India **45**

The Great Wall of China **46**

The Tower, Dubai **31**

Todaiji Temple, Japan **41**

TransAmerica Pyramid, US **34**

Tuntex Sky Tower, Taiwan **20**

Two International Finance Centre, Hong Kong **19**

W

Westend Straße 1, Germany **28**

Woolworth Building, US **10**

30 St. Mary Axe, London **18**